CONTENTS

Introduction: Embrace Wealth as a Journey	4
Chapter 1: Running the Race of Life	7
Chapter 2: The Road Less Traveled: Overcoming Financial Setbacks	10
Chapter 3: Mapping Your Financial Journey	15
Chapter 4: Building a Resilient Financial Foundation	19
Chapter 5: Investing in Your Future	23
Chapter 6: Mastering the Art of Budgeting	27
Chapter 7: Creating Streams of Passive Income	31
Chapter 8: The Power of Financial Mindset	35
Chapter 9: Navigating Financial Risks	39
Chapter 10: Planning for Retirement	43
Chapter 11: Building Generational Wealth	47
Chapter 12: Navigating Financial Challenges Together	51
Chapter 13: Leveraging Community and Networking	55
Chapter 14: Sustaining Wealth Through Mindset	59
Chapter 15: The Power of Giving Back	63
Chapter 16: Embracing Your Financial Journey	67

ROBERT WYATT

Wealth Detours

Copyright © 2024 by Robert Wyatt

All rights reserved. No part of this book may be reproduced or transmitted in any form or by any means without written permission from the author.

INTRODUCTION: EMBRACE WEALTH AS A JOURNEY

Wealth is not just about money or material possessions. It's about the values you live by, the relationships you nurture, and the legacy you leave behind. It's a concept that is inclusive and accessible to everyone, regardless of their starting point. Too often, we equate wealth with a bank account balance or a collection of assets, missing the broader picture of what it means to live abundantly. Wealth, in its truest sense, encompasses every aspect of your life—spiritual, emotional, relational, and financial.

Creating wealth feels distant for many as if it is reserved for a privileged few with more resources, connections, or talent. But that's a misconception. The truth is that wealth is attainable for anyone willing to take intentional steps, embrace wisdom, and rely on faith. It doesn't matter where you begin—what matters is the direction you choose to go from here. Every journey starts with a single step, and this book is your invitation to take that step toward building a meaningful and prosperous life.

My journey toward understanding wealth was not linear. It was filled with detours, missteps, and moments of clarity (I'm still learning). Like many of you, I began with little direction but a lot of ambition. Along the way, I encountered setbacks that taught me valuable lessons about perseverance and intentionality. I realized that the road to wealth is less about achieving perfection and more about consistently progressing. No matter how small, each choice contributes to the legacy you leave behind.

One of my most significant lessons is that wealth is deeply tied to your mindset. If you believe wealth is only for others, you've already limited yourself. But if you approach life with the belief that you can build something meaningful, you open yourself to opportunities you may have never considered. This shift in perspective requires courage, but it's the first step toward transforming your life.

Another essential truth is that wealth, as we see it in this book, is about stewardship. Stewardship means managing your resources wisely, making decisions that align with your values, and prioritizing what truly matters. It's about creating something that benefits you and uplifts those around you. Everything we have-our time, resources, and talents-is a gift from God. How we use those gifts defines the impact we make.

Faith plays a critical role in the journey to wealth. Trusting in God's plan allows you to move forward confidently, even when the path is uncertain. Faith provides the resilience needed to overcome obstacles and the clarity to make decisions rooted in purpose. It's a guiding force that can help you build a foundation for a fulfilling and impactful life.

This book is not about quick fixes or shortcuts. It's not about accumulating riches for the sake of appearances. Instead, it's about creating sustainable wealth that enriches your life and leaves a lasting legacy. Throughout these pages, I share insights and strategies that have helped me and others navigate life's financial and personal detours. These lessons inspire you to take control of your journey.

We often underestimate the power of small, consistent actions. Whether setting aside a portion of your income for savings, nurturing relationships, or committing to daily prayer and reflection, these actions compound over time. They create the momentum needed to achieve your goals and build a life of abundance. It's a reminder that every small step you take is a significant contribution to your journey.

As you read this book, I encourage you to approach it with an open mind and a teachable spirit. Reflect on your experiences and consider how the lessons apply to your unique circumstances. This is not a one-size-fits-all guide; it's a framework to help you discover what wealth means to you and how to attain it.

The journey to wealth is not without challenges but worth every step. Each choice brings you closer to a life that reflects your values and purpose. Remember, the most critical step is the first one—the decision to begin. Once you take that step, you'll find that the path becomes more apparent with each moment of intentionality.

As you turn these pages, let this book be a companion on your journey. Allow it to challenge and inspire you to think differently about wealth and what it means to live a prosperous life. Let it remind you that wealth is not just about what you gain but what you create, give, and leave behind.

This is your moment. Take the first step. Your legacy awaits.

CHAPTER 1: RUNNING THE RACE OF LIFE

Life is often described as a race, but the type of race we imagine can vary greatly. In my youth, I viewed life as a sprint—a quick dash to prove my abilities and secure success as fast as possible. I focused on power, speed, and showing others what I could achieve. But as I grew older and wiser, I realized life is much more like a marathon, requiring endurance, direction, and purpose. The sprinter's approach burned me, and I was disillusioned, while the marathon mindset taught me the value of pacing myself and staying the course.

The Bible provides profound wisdom on this topic. Ecclesiastes 9:11 reminds us, "The race is not to the swift, nor the battle to the strong, neither yet bread to the wise, nor yet riches to men of understanding, nor yet favor to men of skill; but time and chance happeneth to them all." This verse underscores the reality that talent, strength, or intelligence alone does not guarantee success. It often depends on timing, opportunity, and divine purpose. Life humbles us in this way, reminding us of the limitations of our control.

As a young man, I was ambitious, but my choices lacked focus. I chased accolades, material wealth, and the approval of others, only to find these pursuits left me feeling empty. I wasted time trying to outrun others instead of reaching a meaningful goal. I learned the hard way that when we run aimlessly, we risk exhausting ourselves for rewards that do not satisfy.

Time is our most precious resource, yet it is often the most underestimated. In our youth, we believe we have endless time to achieve our dreams and correct our mistakes. This illusion can lead to procrastination and wasted opportunities. As I grew older, I realized how finite time truly is. Each moment wasted is a moment we can never recover. This realization changed my perspective, making me more intentional about how I spend my time.

Unlike time, other resources—money, energy, and relationships—can often be replenished. This difference should compel us to prioritize our time with urgency and purpose. Every decision we make, and every step we take contributes to the legacy we leave behind. Understanding this has been one of the most transformative lessons of my life. It has taught me to focus on what truly matters and to let go of distractions that do not align with my values.

Life's detours often appear as setbacks but can ultimately guide us toward greater understanding. I've had my share of detours—promising pursuits that ended in disappointment. Yet, these experiences were not wasted. They taught me resilience, humility, and the importance of aligning my actions with my purpose. When viewed through the lens of faith, detours are opportunities for growth.

Another key lesson is recognizing the interconnectedness of our choices. Every decision creates a ripple effect, influencing not only our own lives but also the lives of those around us. I've seen how sabotaging others for personal gain can backfire unexpectedly. Building strong, positive relationships and maintaining integrity in our actions are essential for lasting success.

Endurance is a quality we often overlook in the race of life. While the swift may tire and the strong may falter, those who remain steady and purposeful are the ones who persevere. Endurance is not just about physical stamina but about cultivating the mental and spiritual strength to keep moving forward, even when the journey is challenging. It requires discipline, patience, and trust in God's timing.

Success in life's race is not measured solely by wealth or status but by aligning our actions with divine principles. When we run with wisdom and faith, we discover wealth transcending material possessions. We find purpose, fulfillment, and the joy of knowing we are on the right path. This perspective has redefined my understanding of what it means to succeed.

As you reflect on your race, consider the direction you are heading and the choices you are making. Are they leading you closer to your purpose? Are you pacing yourself for the long journey or sprinting toward temporary rewards? The answers to these questions will shape the legacy you leave behind.

The race of life is unique for each of us, but the principles that guide us are universal. By focusing on endurance, wisdom, and faith, we can confidently navigate the detours and obstacles. Life may not always go according to plan, but when we trust in God's purpose, we can be assured that we are exactly where we need to be.

This chapter invites you to assess your race and recalibrate if necessary. It's never too late to change direction, to slow down, or to pick up the pace. Life's marathon requires intention, perseverance, and the willingness to grow with every step. The journey is worth it because the destination is a life well-lived.

conversation humbly and gracefully. May our words glorify You and bless those around us. In Jesus' name, Amen.

CHAPTER 2: THE ROAD LESS TRAVELED: OVERCOMING FINANCIAL SETBACKS

Financial setbacks are like unexpected roadblocks on a journey; they force you to pause, reassess, and often take a detour. Yet, these roadblocks can offer hidden opportunities—moments to reevaluate priorities, discover new pathways, and emerge stronger. These detours can feel frustrating, even insurmountable, but they also hold opportunities to learn and grow. This chapter will explore how to navigate through financial challenges, recover from setbacks, and build a solid foundation for your financial future.

Understanding Financial Setbacks

Financial setbacks come in many forms: job loss, medical expenses, unexpected home repairs, or even poor financial decisions. For many, these challenges create guilt, shame, or hopelessness. The first step in overcoming them is acknowledging that setbacks are normal in life. They do not define you; your response to them does.

Reflecting on past challenges can offer valuable lessons. For instance, if you experienced a job loss, consider how you managed your expenses or sought new opportunities. How did you handle the situation emotionally and financially? What strategies worked, and what would you approach differently now? These reflections provide insights and empower you to make better choices moving forward.

Embracing a Growth Mindset

Adopting a growth mindset is one of the most powerful tools for overcoming setbacks. This perspective shifts your focus from "Why did this happen to me?" to "What can I learn from this?" For example, a job loss can be an opportunity to pivot to a more fulfilling career. At the same time, a medical expense might serve as a wake-up call to prioritize health and financial preparedness.

A growth mindset fosters resilience, allowing you to see possibilities rather than limitations. To cultivate this mindset, focus on daily affirmations, seek out stories of others who have overcome financial challenges, and remind yourself that setbacks are temporary stages on the growth path. It encourages creative problem-solving, helping you identify new ways to earn, save, and invest.

Assessing Your Financial Situation

When facing a setback, it's essential to take a clear-eyed view of your financial situation. Start by listing your income, expenses, and debts. This exercise may feel daunting, but it's a critical step toward regaining control.

- Income: Are there ways to increase your income temporarily, such as taking on a side job or selling unused items?
- Expenses: Which expenses are essential, and where can you cut back?
- Debt: How can you prioritize paying off high-interest debt while managing necessary costs?

Creating a detailed budget based on this assessment will

provide a roadmap to help you move forward. For example, allocate specific percentages of your income to categories such as savings, debt repayment, and essentials, ensuring a clear and actionable plan.

Leveraging Resources

Many resources are available to help during financial difficulties. These include government assistance programs, nonprofit organizations, and community support groups. Don't hesitate to reach out for help; these resources exist to provide temporary relief and guidance.

Additionally, consider consulting a financial advisor or attending free financial literacy workshops. These experts can offer tailored advice and strategies to help you navigate your challenges.

Building a Financial Safety Net

One of the lessons setbacks teach is the importance of preparation. Once you've stabilized your finances, building an emergency fund should be a top priority. Start small—even setting aside $10 or $20 per week can make a significant difference over time.

A robust safety net also includes insurance. Health, home, auto, and life insurance can protect you from the financial fallout of unforeseen events. Review your policies regularly to ensure they meet your needs.

Turning Setbacks into Opportunities

Every financial setback has the potential to become a turning point. For instance, a credit card debt crisis might inspire you to develop a cash-only spending system, while a job loss could lead to a career change that aligns better with your skills and passions.

Consider the story of Thomas, a man who lost his job during

the economic downturn. Facing uncertainty, Thomas took online courses to enhance his skills and networked extensively within his community. Eventually, he pursued his dream of starting a small business, combining his newfound skills with his passion for helping others. Though the journey was challenging, Thomas eventually built a thriving company, transforming his setback into success. Initially devastated, he used the opportunity to pursue his dream of starting a small business. Though the journey was challenging, Thomas eventually built a thriving company, transforming his setback into success. His story is a reminder that challenges can pave the way for growth and fulfillment.

Action Steps

1. Reflect: Write down one financial setback and the lessons you learned from it.
2. Assess: Create a detailed budget to understand your current financial situation.
3. Plan: Identify one immediate action you can take to improve your financial standing, such as cutting an expense or earning extra income.
4. Prepare: Start building an emergency fund, no matter how small the initial contributions.
5. Seek Support: Research and contact local resources or financial advisors for guidance.

Closing Reflection

Financial detours are rarely easy but offer opportunities to grow stronger and wiser. By embracing a growth mindset, leveraging available resources, and planning for the future, you can turn setbacks into stepping stones toward financial freedom. Remember, the road less traveled often leads to the most rewarding destinations.

Take a moment to reflect on this: What detours have shaped your financial journey, and how can they guide your next steps?

Inspirational Thought

"Success is not final, failure is not fatal: It is the courage to continue that count." —Winston Churchill.

CHAPTER 3: MAPPING YOUR FINANCIAL JOURNEY

Every journey requires a map, and your financial journey is no different. A clear, well-thought-out financial plan is your guide to achieving your goals and avoiding unnecessary detours. This chapter will discuss defining your financial goals, creating a roadmap to reach them, and staying on course through life's inevitable twists and turns.

Defining Your Financial Goals

The first step to mapping your financial journey is setting clear and measurable goals. Goals give your plan direction and purpose, helping you prioritize what matters most. Start by categorizing your goals into short-term, medium-term, and long-term objectives:

- Short-term goals include building an emergency fund, paying off credit card debt, or saving for a vacation.
- Medium-term goals involve buying a home, starting a business, or investing in further education.
- Long-term goals often focus on retirement savings, creating a legacy, or achieving financial independence.

For each goal, define a specific timeline and amount. For example, instead of saying, "I want to save money," say, "I want to save $10,000 for a home down payment within three years." This clarity provides motivation and a clear target to work toward.

Creating Your Financial Roadmap

Once you have defined your goals, it's time to create a roadmap. Think of this as your financial GPS, guiding you step by step toward your destination. Follow these steps to build your roadmap:

1. Assess Your Starting Point: Begin by understanding your current financial situation. Review your income, expenses, debts, and assets. Knowing where you stand is essential to charting a realistic path forward.
2. Break Down Your Goals: Divide each financial goal into smaller, manageable steps. For instance, if your goal is to save $10,000, determine how much you need to save monthly or weekly to reach that amount within your timeline.
3. Prioritize Your Goals: Focus on high-impact goals first, such as building an emergency fund or paying off high-interest debt. These priorities lay the foundation for achieving more significant goals in the future.
4. Develop a Budget: Create a budget that aligns with your goals. Allocate a portion of your income toward savings, investments, and debt repayment. Remember, your budget is a flexible tool that can adapt as your circumstances change.
5. Set Milestones: Celebrate progress by setting milestones along the way. For example, reaching your first $1,000 in savings or paying off a significant portion of debt deserves acknowledgment and reinforcement.

Staying Flexible

Life rarely goes according to plan, and your financial journey will likely encounter unexpected challenges. Staying flexible and adapting your roadmap is not just a strategy, it's a mindset, crucial to overcoming these obstacles. Regularly review your financial plan to ensure it remains relevant and aligned with your goals. Remember, it's not about the plan, it's about your ability to adjust and keep moving forward.

Consider the story of Maria, who planned to save $20,000 for a down payment on a home. Halfway through her journey, an unexpected medical expense required her to dip into her savings. Rather than abandoning her goal, Maria adjusted her timeline and budget, demonstrating resilience and adaptability. Ultimately, she achieved her goal a few months later than planned.

Leveraging Technology and Tools

Technology can be a powerful ally in managing your finances and staying on track. Use budgeting apps, financial calculators, and goal-tracking tools to simplify the process. These tools can provide insights, reminders, and visual representations of your progress, making it easier to stay motivated.

Some popular options include:

- Budgeting Apps: Mint, YNAB (You Need A Budget), and EveryDollar.
- Investment Tools: Robinhood, Acorns, and Betterment.
- Goal Trackers: Personal spreadsheets or apps like Goalsetter and Habitica.

Building Accountability

Accountability is a critical component of any financial journey. Share your goals with a trusted friend, family member, or financial advisor who can provide encouragement and hold you accountable. Regular check-ins with your accountability partner can help you stay focused and motivated.

Consider joining a financial accountability group or community. These groups offer a supportive environment where members share tips, celebrate successes, and navigate challenges together.

Action Steps

1. Set Goals: Write down three financial goals, including timelines and amounts.
2. Create a Plan: Break each goal into actionable steps and incorporate them.

CHAPTER 4: BUILDING A RESILIENT FINANCIAL FOUNDATION

A strong foundation is the cornerstone of any lasting structure, and the same is true for your financial well-being. Without a stable base, the weight of unforeseen challenges or opportunities can topple even the most carefully crafted plans. This chapter focuses on building a resilient financial foundation to withstand life's uncertainties and support your long-term goals.

Establishing an Emergency Fund

An emergency fund is your first line of defense against financial instability. It acts as a safety net, providing peace of mind and preventing you from falling into debt when unexpected expenses arise. Here's how to start building one:

1. Set a Target: Aim for three to six months' essential living expenses. If that seems overwhelming, start smaller—even $500 can make a big difference.
2. Automate Savings: Set up automatic transfers to a dedicated savings account. Consistency is key, even if the amount is small.
3. Reduce Nonessential Spending: Identify areas where you can cut back temporarily to prioritize your emergency

fund.
4. **Avoid Temptation:** Keep your emergency fund separate from your regular accounts to reduce the likelihood of dipping into it for non-emergencies.

Managing Debt Effectively

Debt can be a tool or a burden, depending on how it's managed. To build a resilient foundation, focus on reducing high-interest debt and using Credit wisely:

- Prioritize High-Interest Debt: Pay down credit card balances and other high-interest loans first, as they can quickly spiral out of control.
- Consolidate or Refinance: Explore options to lower interest rates or combine multiple debts into a manageable payment.
- Use Credit Strategically: Avoid unnecessary debt and only borrow for investments that enhance your financial standing, such as education or homeownership.
- Track Your Progress: Regularly review your debt repayment plan to stay motivated and make adjustments as needed.

Diversifying Income Streams

Relying on a single source of income can leave you vulnerable during economic downturns or personal setbacks. Diversifying your income increases your financial stability and opens up new opportunities for growth. Consider these strategies:

- Side Hustles: Start a small business, freelance, or take on part-time work in an area that interests you.
- Passive Income: Explore investments like rental properties, dividend-paying stocks, or peer-to-peer lending.
- Skill Development: Invest in education or training to

qualify for higher-paying roles or new career paths.

Protecting Your Assets

Insurance is a critical component of a resilient financial foundation. It shields you from catastrophic losses and provides a safety net for your loved ones. Key types of insurance include:

- Health Insurance: Covers medical expenses and protects against unexpected healthcare costs.
- Life Insurance: Ensures your family's financial security during your passing.
- Home and Auto Insurance: Safeguards your property and vehicles from damage or theft.
- Disability Insurance: Replaces income if you're unable to work due to illness or injury.

Review your insurance policies annually to ensure they meet your current needs and adjust coverage as necessary.

Building Financial Literacy

Knowledge is power, and financial literacy equips you to make informed decisions. Continuously educating yourself on personal finance topics can help you navigate complex situations and avoid costly mistakes. Here are some ways to boost your financial knowledge:

- Read Books and Articles: Find reputable budgeting, investing, and financial planning resources.
- Attend Workshops: Participate in community or online seminars focused on financial education.
- Follow Experts: Subscribe to trusted financial advisors' podcasts, blogs, or social media accounts.
- Practice What You Learn: Apply new concepts to your financial situation to gain practical experience.

Action Steps

1. Start Saving: Open a dedicated emergency fund account

and set up automatic transfers.
2. **Tackle Debt**: Create a plan to pay off high-interest debt and track your progress.
3. **Explore Income Opportunities**: Identify one way to diversify your income and take the first step toward implementing it.
4. **Review Insurance**: Evaluate your current policies and make adjustments if needed.
5. **Educate Yourself**: Commit to reading one financial book or attending a workshop in the next month.

Closing Reflection

Building a resilient financial foundation is an investment in your future. It requires effort, discipline, and a proactive approach, but the rewards are worth it. A strong foundation provides stability and gives you the confidence to pursue your dreams without fear of financial collapse.

Take a moment to reflect on this: What steps can you take today to strengthen your financial foundation?

Inspirational Thought

"Do not wait until the conditions are perfect to begin. Beginning makes the conditions perfect." —Alan Cohen.

CHAPTER 5: INVESTING IN YOUR FUTURE

Investing is more than just a financial strategy; it is a powerful commitment to your future self. It empowers you to grow your wealth, achieve your long-term goals, and secure financial independence. This chapter will introduce the fundamentals of investing, explore various types of investments, and provide practical tips to help you begin or refine your investment journey.

Why Investing Matters

Saving alone is often insufficient to build significant wealth due to inflation and rising living costs. Investing allows you to grow your money faster, enabling you to achieve goals such as retirement, homeownership, or funding education. It also helps you build passive income streams, creating financial stability and freedom.

Understanding Investment Basics

Before diving into specific investment options, it's essential to understand key concepts that will guide your decisions:

- Risk vs. Reward: Higher-risk investments typically offer greater potential returns but also have a higher chance of loss. Balancing your portfolio based on your risk tolerance is crucial.

- Time Horizon: The time you plan to invest impacts your choices. Short-term goals may require conservative investments, while long-term goals allow more aggressive strategies.
- Diversification: Spreading your investments across different asset classes minimizes risk and increases the potential for stable returns.
- Compounding: Reinvesting your earnings allows your investments to grow exponentially over time.

Types of Investments

There are numerous ways to invest, each with its benefits and risks. Below are some of the most common options:

1. Stocks: Investing in companies through stock purchases provides the potential for high returns but comes with market volatility.
2. Bonds: These fixed-income investments offer lower risk and steady returns, making them ideal for conservative investors.
3. Mutual Funds and ETFs: These pooled investment vehicles provide instant diversification and are managed by professionals.
4. Real Estate: Property investment can generate rental income and long-term appreciation but requires significant upfront capital.
5. Retirement Accounts: Options like 401(k)s and IRAs offer tax advantages and are essential for long-term financial planning.
6. Alternative Investments: Cryptocurrencies, art, and commodities can provide high returns but often come with higher risk and less predictability.

Steps to Start Investing

1. Set Clear Goals: Define what you want to achieve through investing, whether saving for retirement,

buying a home, or growing wealth.
2. **Build a Strong Foundation:** Ensure you have an emergency fund and manageable debt levels before investing.
3. **Educate Yourself:** Research investment options, terms, and strategies to make informed decisions.
4. **Start Small:** Begin with a modest amount and increase your contributions as you gain confidence and experience.
5. **Leverage Technology:** Use investment apps or robo-advisors to simplify the process and access diversified portfolios.
6. **Seek Professional Guidance:** Consult with a financial advisor for personalized advice or help creating an investment plan.

Overcoming Common Investment Challenges

Many people hesitate to invest due to fear, lack of knowledge, or financial constraints. Here's how to address these challenges:

- **Fear of Loss:** Start with low-risk investments and gradually explore higher-risk options as you become more comfortable.
- **Knowledge Gaps:** Use free resources, such as online courses, books, and webinars, to build your confidence.
- **Limited Funds:** Begin with micro-investing platforms that allow you to invest small amounts, such as Acorns or Stash.

The Power of Consistency

Consistency is one of the most important factors in successful investing. Regular contributions, even in small amounts, can lead to significant growth over time. For example, investing $200 per month in a diversified portfolio with a 7% annual return could grow to over $48,000 in 10 years, showing the potential for your investments to blossom.

Action Steps

1. Research Options: Choose one or two investment types to learn about in-depth.
2. Set Up an Account: Open an investment account, such as a brokerage or retirement account.
3. Start Investing: Commit to a specific amount each month and automate contributions.
4. Track Progress: Monitor your portfolio regularly and adjust based on your goals and market conditions.
5. Keep Learning: Dedicate time each month to expanding your investment knowledge.

Closing Reflection

Investing in your future is one of the most empowering steps toward financial independence. While the journey may seem daunting initially, a steady and informed approach will yield rewards over time. Remember, every small step you take today lays the groundwork for a more secure and abundant tomorrow.

Take a moment to reflect: What investment choices align with your goals and values, and how can you start acting on them today?

Inspirational Thought

"The best investment you can make is in yourself." —Warren Buffett.

CHAPTER 6: MASTERING THE ART OF BUDGETING

Budgeting is the backbone of financial success. It's a powerful tool that allows you to take control of your money, reduce stress, and achieve your financial goals with confidence. In this chapter, we will delve into the essentials of budgeting, explore different methods, and provide practical tips for making budgeting a sustainable and rewarding habit.

Why Budgeting Matters

A budget is more than just a list of numbers; it reflects your priorities and a roadmap to achieving your dreams. Budgeting helps you:

- Understand Your Finances: Gain a clear picture of your income and expenses.
- Control Spending: Avoid overspending and identify areas where you can save.
- Achieve Goals: Allocate resources toward savings, investments, and debt repayment.
- Reduce Financial Stress: Eliminate the guesswork from managing money.

Steps to Create an Effective Budget

1. Calculate Your Income: Start by determining your total monthly income, including salary, side hustle earnings,

and any other sources.
2. **Track Your Expenses:** Record all expenses for at least one month to understand where your money goes. Categorize them into fixed (e.g., rent, utilities) and variable (e.g., groceries, entertainment) expenses.
3. **Set Priorities:** Align your spending with your goals. Focus on essentials and allocate remaining funds to savings, investments, and discretionary spending.
4. **Choose a Budgeting Method:** Select a budgeting approach that suits your lifestyle and financial situation (see next section).
5. **Please review and Adjust:** Revisit your budget regularly to ensure it aligns with your goals and circumstances.

Popular Budgeting Methods

There is no one-size-fits-all approach to budgeting. Experiment with different methods to find what works best for you:

- **50/30/20 Rule:** Allocate 50% of your income to needs, 30% to wants, and 20% to savings and debt repayment.
- **Zero-Based Budgeting:** Assign every dollar a job, ensuring your income minus expenses equals zero.
- **Envelope System:** Use cash for specific categories, such as groceries and entertainment, and stop spending once the envelope is empty.
- **Pay-Yourself-First Method:** Dedicate a portion of your income to savings and investments before covering other expenses.
- **Percentage-Based Budgeting:** Divide income into fixed percentages based on your priorities (e.g., 60% living expenses, 20% savings, 10% investments, 10% fun).

Tools to Simplify Budgeting

Technology can make budgeting more straightforward and more efficient. Use apps or software to track expenses, set goals, and monitor progress. Popular options include:

- Mint: Provides a comprehensive overview of your finances.
- YNAB (You Need A Budget): Focuses on giving every dollar a purpose.
- EveryDollar: Simplifies budgeting with a zero-based approach.
- Personal Capital: Combines budgeting with investment tracking.
- Spreadsheets: Create a customized budget using tools like Google Sheets or Excel.

Overcoming Budgeting Challenges

Many people struggle to stick to a budget due to common challenges. Here are strategies to address them:

- Irregular Income: Base your budget on an average or minimum income level and adjust for months with higher earnings.
- Unexpected Expenses: Build a buffer or emergency fund into your budget.
- Lack of Discipline: Automate payments and savings to reduce the temptation to overspend.
- Feeling Restricted: Allow for occasional splurges within your budget to maintain motivation.

The Rewards of Budgeting

The benefits of budgeting extend far beyond financial health. It fosters discipline, clarity, and a sense of accomplishment. Over time, consistent budgeting habits can lead to:

- Improved Savings: Grow your emergency fund and investments.
- Debt Freedom: Pay off loans and credit card balances faster.
- Financial Independence: Achieve the freedom to make choices without financial constraints.

- Reduced Stress: Gain peace of mind knowing you control your money.

Action Steps

1. Start Small: Begin with a simple budget for one month.
2. Track Expenses: Use an app or spreadsheet to categorize your spending.
3. Set a Goal: Choose one financial goal and allocate resources toward it.
4. Experiment: Try different budgeting methods to find your best fit.
5. Review Monthly: Schedule a regular time to update and adjust your budget.

Closing Reflection

Budgeting is not about deprivation; it's about empowerment. By mastering the art of budgeting, you can direct your financial resources with intention and purpose. This simple yet powerful habit can transform your financial life and help you achieve the most important goals.

Take a moment to reflect: How can creating a budget help you align your finances with your values and dreams? Budgeting is not just about numbers, it's about making your money work for what truly matters to you.

Inspirational Thought

"A budget is telling your money where to go instead of wondering where it went." —Dave Ramsey.

CHAPTER 7: CREATING STREAMS OF PASSIVE INCOME

Passive income is the key to financial freedom. Unlike active income, which requires continuous effort, passive income allows you to earn money with minimal ongoing involvement. This chapter will explore various ways to generate passive income, its benefits, and how to get started.

Why Passive Income Matters

Relying solely on active income can limit your financial growth and independence. Passive income provides:

- Financial Security: Diversifies your earnings, reducing reliance on a single source.
- Time Freedom: You can focus on what matters most without constant work demands.
- Wealth Building: This creates opportunities to reinvest and grow your financial portfolio.

Types of Passive Income Streams

There are many ways to generate passive income, each with the required level of effort and investment. Here are some popular options:

1. Real Estate Investments:
    - Rental Properties: Earn monthly income

by leasing out residential or commercial properties.
- REITs (Real Estate Investment Trusts): Invest in real estate portfolios without owning physical properties.

2. Dividend Stocks:
   - Purchase shares in companies that distribute regular dividends, providing a steady income stream.
3. Peer-to-Peer Lending:
   - Use platforms like LendingClub or Prosper to earn interest by lending money to individuals or businesses.
4. Digital Products:
   - Create eBooks, courses, or templates and sell them online through platforms like Amazon, Gumroad, or Teachable.
5. Affiliate Marketing:
   - Promote products or services through your blog, website, or social media and earn a commission on sales.
6. Royalties:
   - Earn royalties from creative work such as books, music, or software.
7. Automated Online Businesses:
   - Build a dropshipping store or subscription-based service that requires minimal day-to-day management.
8. Investment Accounts:
   - Utilize high-yield savings accounts, CDs, or index funds for stable, low-risk returns.

Getting Started with Passive Income

Creating passive income streams requires planning, effort, and initial investment. Follow these steps to get started:

1. Assess Your Resources: Determine how much time, money, and skills you can invest upfront.
2. Choose a Stream: Select one or two passive income options that align with your interests and resources.
3. Research: Learn the basics of your chosen stream through books, courses, or expert advice.
4. Take Action: Begin small to minimize risk and gain experience. For instance, start with a single rental property or create one digital product.
5. Automate: Use technology and systems to reduce manual effort and scale your income streams over time.
6. Monitor and Adjust: Review your passive income sources regularly to optimize performance and address challenges.

Overcoming Challenges

While passive income is rewarding, it's not without challenges. Here's how to address common obstacles:

- Initial Investment: Start with low-cost options like affiliate marketing or dividend stocks if funds are limited.
- Time Constraints: Dedicate a few hours weekly to building and maintaining your passive income sources.
- Skill Gaps: Invest in learning through courses or mentorships to acquire the skills needed for success.

The Power of Compounding

One of the greatest advantages of passive income is its potential to compound over time. For example, reinvesting dividends or rental income into additional shares or properties can significantly accelerate your wealth-building efforts. Patience and consistency are key to reaping long-term rewards.

Action Steps

1. Identify Opportunities: Write down three passive income streams you want to pursue.
2. Create a Plan: Outline the steps needed to start each stream, including costs and timelines.
3. Invest in Education: Dedicate time to learning about your chosen streams before diving in.
4. Start Small: Launch one passive income stream and gradually expand as you gain experience.
5. Track Progress: Monitor your earnings and reinvest to grow your income over time.

Closing Reflection

Building passive income streams is a powerful way to achieve financial freedom and security. While it requires effort upfront, the long-term benefits are well worth it. With careful planning and persistence, you can create a life where your money works for you instead of vice versa.

Take a moment to reflect: What steps can you take today to start building your first stream of passive income?

Inspirational Thought

"Don't work for money; make money work for you." —Robert Kiyosaki.

CHAPTER 8: THE POWER OF FINANCIAL MINDSET

Your mindset is the foundation of your financial success. It influences how you view money, make decisions, and overcome challenges. Developing a healthy and growth-oriented financial mindset can transform your approach to wealth creation and enable you to achieve your goals. This chapter will explore the components of a strong financial mindset, strategies to cultivate it, and how to use it to fuel your financial journey.

Understanding Your Financial Mindset

Your beliefs, experiences, and habits shape your financial mindset. It impacts how you:

- Set Goals: Ambitious or modest, your mindset determines your level of aspiration.
- Take Risks: A positive mindset encourages calculated risks, while a fear-driven one may hinder opportunities.
- Handle Setbacks: A resilient mindset helps you bounce back stronger after challenges.
- View Money: Whether you see money as a tool for growth or a source of stress often depends on your mindset.

Shifting from Scarcity to Abundance

Shifting from Scarcity to Abundance: Liberating Your Financial

Potential
To make this shift:

1. Reframe Negative Thoughts: Replace "I can't afford this" with "How can I make this possible?"
2. Celebrate Small Wins: Recognize progress, no matter how small, to build confidence.
3. Focus on Possibilities: Visualize your goals and the steps to achieve them rather than dwelling on obstacles.

Cultivating Financial Discipline

Discipline is a critical aspect of a strong financial mindset. It requires setting clear boundaries, making deliberate choices, and staying consistent. Strategies to enhance financial discipline include:

- Automating Savings: Redirect a portion of your income into savings or investments before spending.
- Tracking Progress: Regularly review your financial goals and adjust as needed.
- Delaying Gratification: Practice waiting before making non-essential purchases to ensure alignment with your priorities.

Overcoming Limiting Beliefs

Limiting beliefs such as "I'm not good with money" or "I'll never be wealthy" can sabotage your financial progress. To overcome these beliefs:

1. Identify the Root Cause: Reflect on experiences or messages that shaped these beliefs.
2. Challenge the Belief: Question its validity and seek evidence to the contrary.
3. Replace with Empowering Beliefs: Adopt affirmations like "I am capable of managing money wisely" or "I have the power to create wealth."

Building Resilience

Financial resilience is adapting and thriving in the face of challenges. It's cultivated through:

- Emergency Planning: Prepare for unexpected events with an emergency fund and insurance.
- Continuous Learning: Stay informed about financial trends and opportunities.
- Support Systems: Surround yourself with mentors, friends, and communities encouraging positive financial behaviors.

Leveraging Gratitude

Gratitude shifts your focus from what you lack to what you have, fostering contentment and reducing impulsive spending. Incorporate gratitude into your financial routine by:

- Keeping a gratitude journal to document financial progress and blessings.
- Celebrating milestones, no matter how small.
- Acknowledging the resources and opportunities that contribute to your success.

Action Steps

1. Assess Your Mindset: Write down your beliefs about money and identify which ones serve you and which do not.
2. Adopt Affirmations: Create three empowering financial affirmations and recite them daily.
3. Practice Gratitude: List five things you're grateful for about your finances.
4. Set a Discipline Goal: Choose one financial habit to implement or strengthen this month.
5. Reflect on Progress: Schedule regular check-ins to evaluate and refine your mindset.

Closing Reflection

Your financial mindset is a powerful tool that shapes every aspect of your wealth journey. By cultivating a positive and resilient perspective, you can navigate challenges, seize opportunities, and achieve lasting success. Remember, how you think about money determines how it works for you.

Take a moment to reflect: How can shifting your mindset unlock new possibilities for your financial future?

Inspirational Thought

"Whether you think you can, or you think you can't—you're right."
—Henry Ford

CHAPTER 9: NAVIGATING FINANCIAL RISKS

Every financial decision comes with a degree of risk, but understanding and managing those risks can empower you, safeguard your wealth, and help you make informed choices. This chapter will explore the types of financial risks, strategies to mitigate them, and how to turn risks into opportunities.

Understanding Financial Risks

Financial risks can arise from various sources, including market fluctuations, personal circumstances, and unforeseen events. Common types include:

1. Market Risk: The potential for losses due to changes in market conditions, such as stock market volatility or interest rate fluctuations.
2. Credit Risk: The risk of borrowers failing to repay loans or fulfill financial obligations.
3. Liquidity Risk: The inability to access cash or sell investments when needed without incurring significant losses.
4. Inflation Risk: The diminishing purchasing power of money over time due to rising prices.
5. Personal Risk: Financial challenges stemming from job loss, health issues, or family emergencies.

The Importance of Risk Management

Risk management is about protecting your assets and recovering from setbacks. A proactive approach reduces the likelihood of significant losses and builds financial resilience. Key benefits include:

- Peace of Mind: Confidence in your financial stability.
- Goal Protection: Ensures your savings and investments are not derailed.
- Opportunity Identification: Helps you recognize and act on calculated risks.

Strategies to Manage Financial Risks

1. Diversification:
   - Spread investments across different asset classes, industries, and geographic regions to minimize exposure to any single risk.
2. Emergency Fund:
   - Maintain a fund with three to six months' living expenses to cover unexpected costs.
3. Insurance:
   - Protect yourself with appropriate policies, such as health, life, disability, and property insurance.
4. Debt Management:
   - Avoid excessive debt and focus on paying off high-interest loans to reduce financial vulnerability.
5. Risk Assessment Tools:
   - Use tools like risk calculators or consult with financial advisors to evaluate potential risks and plan accordingly.

Turning Risks Into Opportunities

While risks seem daunting, they also present opportunities for growth and profit when approached strategically. For example:

- Investing During Market Downturns: Economic recessions often create opportunities to buy undervalued assets that can yield significant returns over time.
- Starting a Business: While risky, entrepreneurship can offer financial independence and growth if carefully planned.
- Exploring New Markets: Diversifying income streams through international investments or emerging industries can provide high-reward opportunities.

Learning from Financial Setbacks

Setbacks are inevitable but can be valuable learning experiences. Reflecting on past financial mistakes helps you identify patterns and make better decisions in the future. Steps to turn setbacks into learning opportunities include:

- Evaluate: Analyze what went wrong and why.
- Adapt: Implement changes to avoid repeating the same mistakes.
- Seek Guidance: Consult experts or mentors for insights and support.

Building a Financial Safety Net

Creating a robust safety net is essential for mitigating risks. Components include:

- Savings: Regular contributions to savings accounts or low-risk investments.
- Insurance: Comprehensive coverage tailored to your specific needs.
- Backup Plans: Contingency strategies for career changes, health issues, or economic downturns.

Action Steps

1. Identify Risks: List the financial risks most relevant to your situation and assess their potential impact.
2. Diversify: Review your portfolio and ensure it is well-diversified.
3. Review Insurance Policies: Confirm that your coverage aligns with your needs.
4. Build a Safety Net: Strengthen your emergency fund and savings.
5. Learn From Setbacks: Reflect on a past financial mistake and outline what you would do differently.

Closing Reflection

Financial risks are inherent in wealth-building, but they don't have to be feared. With careful planning and proactive strategies, you can navigate risks confidently and turn challenges into opportunities. Remember, it's not about avoiding risks entirely but managing them wisely.

Take a moment to reflect: What steps can you take today to better prepare for financial risks?

Inspirational Thought

"In investing, what is comfortable is rarely profitable." —Robert Arnott.

CHAPTER 10: PLANNING FOR RETIREMENT

Retirement planning is one of the most significant financial milestones you will face. It requires a thoughtful approach to maintain your desired lifestyle, cover healthcare costs, and enjoy financial independence in your later years. In this chapter, we will explore the essentials of retirement planning, key strategies to maximize savings, and how to create a plan that works for you.

Why Retirement Planning Matters

Without a clear retirement plan, you risk running out of money or sacrificing your quality of life. Planning allows you to:

- Secure Financial Stability: Ensure your income meets your retirement needs.
- Achieve Peace of Mind: Reduce stress by having a clear path to financial independence.
- Maintain Lifestyle Choices: Support your desired standard of living without compromise.

Assessing Retirement Needs

Understanding how much you'll need for retirement is the first step in planning. Consider these factors:

1. Living Expenses: Estimate monthly costs, including housing, food, transportation, and leisure activities.

2. Healthcare Costs: Account for medical expenses, including insurance premiums, co-pays, and long-term care.
3. Inflation: Adjust for the rising cost of goods and services over time.
4. Life Expectancy: Plan for a retirement that may last 20-30 years or more.

Building a Retirement Savings Plan

A robust savings plan is the cornerstone of retirement planning. Strategies include:

1. Start Early: Save immediately to take advantage of compound interest.
2. Maximize Employer Benefits: Contribute to your 401(k) or similar employer-sponsored plans, especially if your employer offers matching contributions.
3. Use Tax-Advantaged Accounts: Utilize IRAs, Roth IRAs, and HSAs to reduce tax burdens and grow savings.
4. Diversify Investments: Spread investments across stocks, bonds, and other asset classes to balance growth and risk.
5. Automate Contributions: Set up automatic transfers to retirement accounts to ensure consistent savings.

Creating Income Streams for Retirement

In addition to savings, consider creating income streams to support your retirement:

- Social Security: Understand your benefits and the optimal time to start claiming.
- Pensions: If applicable, review your pension plan options and payouts.
- Investment Income: Use dividends, interest, and capital gains to generate passive income.
- Annuities: Consider purchasing annuities for guaranteed lifetime income.

- Part-Time Work: Explore opportunities for consulting or part-time roles if desired.

Managing Risks in Retirement

Retirement has unique financial risks, such as outliving your savings or unexpected medical costs. Mitigate these risks by:
- Creating a Budget: Stick to a retirement budget that balances essential expenses and discretionary spending.
- Maintaining Insurance Coverage: Ensure adequate health, life, and long-term care insurance.
- Adjusting Investments: Shift to more conservative investments as you approach retirement age.
- Building an Emergency Fund: Keep a cash reserve for unexpected expenses.

Catching Up on Retirement Savings

It's never too late to take action if you're behind on savings. Steps to catch up include:
- Increasing Contributions: Max out your retirement accounts, including catch-up contributions for those over 50.
- Reducing Expenses: Free up more money for savings by cutting nonessential spending.
- Delaying Retirement: Postponing retirement can significantly increase your savings and Social Security benefits.
- Exploring Side Income: Use side hustles or part-time work to boost savings.

Action Steps

1. Calculate Needs: Estimate how much you'll need for retirement based on your goals and lifestyle.
2. Review Accounts: Assess your current savings and investment accounts.
3. Increase Contributions: Adjust contributions to

maximize your savings potential.
4. Plan Income Streams: Identify additional income sources for retirement.
5. Seek Professional Advice: Consult a financial advisor to create or refine your plan.

Closing Reflection

Planning for retirement is not a one-time event; it's an ongoing process that requires regular adjustments and a proactive mindset. You can build a secure and fulfilling retirement by starting early, staying consistent, and adapting to changes.

Take a moment to reflect: What steps can you take today to ensure a financially stable and enjoyable retirement?

Inspirational Thought

"The question isn't at what age I want to retire, it's at what income." —George Foreman

---

CHAPTER 11: BUILDING GENERATIONAL WEALTH

True financial success extends beyond your lifetime. Building generational wealth ensures that your hard work benefits your loved ones and creates opportunities for future generations. In this chapter, we will explore strategies for creating and preserving wealth, instilling financial literacy, and establishing a legacy that endures.

What Is Generational Wealth?

Generational wealth refers to assets passed down from one generation to the next. These can include:

- Financial Assets: Savings, investments, and retirement accounts.
- Property: Real estate and other tangible assets.
- Businesses: Family-run enterprises or equity stakes in companies.
- Knowledge: Financial literacy and decision-making skills.

Creating generational wealth isn't just about accumulating resources; it's about empowering the next generation with tools to sustain and grow that wealth. This empowerment is a powerful

motivator that can inspire you to take the necessary steps today.
Strategies for Building Generational Wealth

1. Invest in Assets That Appreciate:
   - Focus on investments like real estate, stocks, and businesses that grow in value over time.
   - Diversify your portfolio to balance risk and reward.
2. Prioritize Life Insurance:
   - A comprehensive life insurance policy ensures your family is financially secure in the event of your passing.
3. Start a Family Business:
   - Building a family enterprise can create a lasting source of income and opportunities for future generations.
4. Save for Education:
   - Invest in 529 plans or other education savings accounts to support your children's academic and professional growth.
5. Establish Trusts:
   - Trusts protect your assets from mismanagement and ensure they are distributed according to your wishes.

Teaching Financial Literacy

Passing down wealth is only part of the equation; teaching financial literacy ensures it is preserved and multiplied. Key lessons include:

- Budgeting: Show younger family members how to manage money effectively.
- Saving and Investing: Teach the importance of saving consistently and the basics of investing.
- Entrepreneurship: Encourage creative thinking and problem-solving skills.

- Risk Management: Discuss the importance of insurance and diversification.

Lead by example and involve your family in financial discussions and decisions. This not only builds their confidence and skills but also fosters a sense of connection and unity within the family.

Estate Planning

Estate planning is critical for protecting and distributing your wealth according to your wishes. Steps include:

1. Create a Will: Clearly outline how you want your assets to be allocated.
2. Designate Beneficiaries: Ensure your financial accounts, life insurance, and retirement plans have up-to-date beneficiary designations.
3. Establish Power of Attorney: Assign trusted individuals to make decisions on your behalf if you become incapacitated.
4. Set Up Trusts: Use trusts to minimize taxes, protect assets, and provide clear instructions for their use.
5. Consult a Professional: Work with an estate planning attorney to navigate legal complexities.

Preserving Wealth

To maintain generational wealth, it's essential to:

- Avoid Debt: Teach future generations to live within their means and prioritize saving over borrowing.
- Plan for Taxes: Use tax-efficient strategies to reduce the burden on your heirs.
- Reinvest Earnings: Encourage reinvestment to grow wealth over time.

Creating a Legacy

A meaningful legacy goes beyond financial assets. Consider:

- Family Values: Pass down principles that guide decision-

making and strengthen familial bonds.
- Charitable Contributions: Establish philanthropic efforts that reflect your values and give back to the community.
- Memories and Traditions: Foster connections through shared experiences and traditions that future generations can carry forward.

Action Steps

1. Assess Assets: Evaluate your current financial standing and identify areas to grow generational wealth.
2. Start Conversations: Involve your family in discussions about money and wealth-building strategies.
3. Plan Your Estate: Work with professionals to create a will, trusts, and other legal documents.
4. Teach Financial Literacy: Dedicate time to educating the next generation about managing and growing wealth.
5. Set Goals: Define specific objectives for creating and preserving a legacy.

Closing Reflection

Building generational wealth is about more than accumulating assets; it's about creating a foundation for opportunity, security, and lasting impact. By taking deliberate steps today, you can ensure your legacy benefits those you care about for years to come. Take a moment to reflect: How can you begin creating a financial legacy that aligns with your values and empowers future generations?

Inspirational Thought

"Someone's sitting in the shade today because someone planted a tree a long time ago." —Warren Buffett

CHAPTER 12: NAVIGATING FINANCIAL CHALLENGES TOGETHER

Financial challenges can feel overwhelming, but navigating them with the support of family, friends, or a trusted community can make all the difference. Collaboration fosters resilience, strengthens relationships, and creates opportunities to overcome obstacles more effectively. In this chapter, we will explore the power of teamwork in tackling financial difficulties and strategies for building a supportive network.

The Importance of Shared Responsibility

Facing financial challenges as a team has several advantages:

- Shared Burden: Spreading the responsibility reduces stress and prevents burnout.
- Diverse Perspectives: Different viewpoints can lead to creative problem-solving.
- Accountability: Partners or groups help keep each other on track.
- Strengthened Bonds: Working together toward common goals deepens trust and connection.

Strategies for Collaborative Financial Success

1. Open Communication:
    - Discuss financial challenges openly and honestly with those involved.
    - Set aside time for regular financial check-ins to ensure alignment.
2. Define Roles:
    - Assign clear responsibilities to each person based on their strengths.
    - For example, one person might handle budgeting while another focuses on managing investments.
3. Set Joint Goals:
    - Establish shared objectives, such as paying off debt, saving for a vacation, or building an emergency fund.
    - Break these goals into manageable steps and celebrate milestones together.
4. Share Resources:
    - Pool resources like time, money, or skills to tackle challenges more efficiently.
    - For instance, splitting childcare responsibilities can free up time to pursue income-generating opportunities.
5. Leverage Strengths:
    - Identify individual strengths and use them to benefit the group.
    - For example, a family member with financial expertise can guide investment decisions.

Building a Supportive Network

A strong support system extends beyond the immediate family. Consider these ways to expand your network:

- Community Groups: Join local organizations or online

forums focused on financial education or mutual aid.
- Mentors: Seek advice from experienced individuals who have successfully navigated similar challenges.
- Professional Help: Consult financial advisors, counselors, or coaches for expert guidance.

Overcoming Common Challenges

Collaboration is not without its difficulties. Here's how to address common issues:

- Conflicting Priorities: Find common ground by focusing on shared values and goals.
- Communication Breakdowns: Establish clear expectations and maintain regular updates.
- Uneven Contributions: Acknowledge individual capacities and focus on equitable, not equal, efforts.

The Role of Trust and Transparency

Trust is the cornerstone of any successful collaboration. Build and maintain trust by:

- Being Honest: Share accurate and complete information about finances.
- Respecting Privacy: Balance transparency with respect for personal boundaries.
- Following Through: Commit to and fulfill agreed-upon responsibilities.

Action Steps

1. Identify Your Team: List the people you can rely on for support and involve them in financial discussions.
2. Create a Plan: Develop a shared action plan to address your financial challenges.
3. Schedule Check-Ins: Set regular meetings to review progress and adjust strategies as needed.
4. Leverage Resources: To enhance your efforts, research

community resources, such as financial workshops or support groups.
5. Celebrate Wins: Acknowledge and celebrate progress, no matter how small, to maintain motivation.

Closing Reflection

Navigating financial challenges is rarely easy, but you don't have to go it alone. By fostering open communication, building a strong support network, and working collaboratively, you can overcome obstacles and create a brighter financial future together.

Take a moment to reflect: How can you involve your support network in addressing your financial challenges?

Inspirational Thought

"Alone we can do so little; together we can do so much." —Helen Keller.

CHAPTER 13: LEVERAGING COMMUNITY AND NETWORKING

Your community and professional network can be powerful allies in achieving financial success. By fostering meaningful relationships, sharing resources, and collaborating with others, you can unlock opportunities that might otherwise remain out of reach. This chapter will explore how to build and leverage networks, the importance of giving back, and strategies for creating mutually beneficial connections.

The Value of Networking

Networking isn't just about expanding your contact list and building genuine, reciprocal relationships. Key benefits include:

- Access to Opportunities: Discover job openings, partnerships, or investment prospects.
- Knowledge Sharing: Learn from the experiences and expertise of others.
- Support Systems: Gain encouragement and advice during financial challenges.
- Collaboration: Partner with others to achieve common goals.

Building Your Network

Creating a strong network requires intentional effort and authenticity. Steps to grow your network include:

1. Join Communities:
    - Participate in local organizations, professional associations, or online groups aligned with your interests.
2. Attend Events:
    - Go to industry conferences, workshops, and meetups to connect with like-minded individuals.
3. Utilize Social Media:
    - Leverage platforms like LinkedIn, Twitter, or niche forums to build professional relationships.
4. Engage in Volunteering:
    - Give back to your community while meeting people who share similar values.
5. Seek Mentors:
    - Identify individuals you admire and approach them for guidance and mentorship.

Strengthening Relationships

Building a network is the first step; maintaining and strengthening those connections is equally important. Strategies include:

- Follow-up: Send a thank-you email or message after meeting someone new.
- Offer Value: Share resources, insights, or introductions that benefit others.
- Stay Consistent: Regularly check in with your network to nurture relationships.
- Celebrate Successes: Acknowledge milestones and achievements within your network.

Leveraging Your Network

Once you've built a strong network, it's time to utilize it effectively. Ways to leverage your connections include:

- Seeking Referrals: Ask for introductions to potential employers, clients, or collaborators.
- Gaining Insights: Request advice on career moves, investment opportunities, or business strategies.
- Collaborating on Projects: Partner with others to share resources and achieve mutual goals.
- Finding Support: Lean on your network for guidance and encouragement during challenging times.

The Role of Giving Back

Giving back is a cornerstone of successful networking. You create a cycle of generosity and trust by contributing to your community and helping others succeed. Ways to give back include:

- Mentorship: Guide someone less experienced in your field or community.
- Donations: Support causes that align with your values.
- Sharing Knowledge: Offer free advice, workshops, or educational content.
- Connecting Others: Facilitate introductions between people in your network.

Overcoming Networking Challenges

Networking can feel daunting, especially for those who are introverted or new to professional circles. Here's how to overcome common challenges:

- Start Small: Begin with close friends, colleagues, or local groups before expanding.
- Set Goals: Define what you hope to achieve through networking to stay focused.

- Be Authentic: Approach relationships with genuine interest and sincerity.
- Practice Confidence: Prepare a brief introduction or elevator pitch to ease initial conversations.

Action Steps

1. Identify Communities: List three groups or organizations you'd like to join.
2. Reach Out: Contact someone in your desired field for advice or mentorship.
3. Plan Engagement: Schedule monthly time for networking activities, such as attending events or connecting online.
4. Offer Value: Find a way to contribute to your network through knowledge sharing or introductions.
5. Reflect on Growth: Regularly evaluate how your network has supported your financial journey and look for ways to strengthen it.

Closing Reflection

Leveraging your community and network is not just about personal gain—it's about creating a web of support, opportunity, and mutual growth. By investing time and energy into these connections, you can achieve financial success while uplifting others.

Take a moment to reflect: How can you better utilize your network to support your financial goals and contribute to the success of others?

Inspirational Thought

"Your network is your net worth." —Porter Gale.

CHAPTER 14: SUSTAINING WEALTH THROUGH MINDSET

Creating wealth is only part of the journey; sustaining it requires a disciplined and proactive mindset. A strong financial mindset not only helps you manage your wealth effectively but also enables you to adapt to changing circumstances and avoid common pitfalls. This chapter will explore the habits, attitudes, and strategies supporting long-term financial sustainability.

The Key Elements of a Wealth-Sustaining Mindset

1. Commitment to Growth:
    - View wealth as a dynamic process that requires ongoing learning and adaptation.
    - Stay informed about market trends, economic changes, and new investment opportunities.
2. Financial Discipline:
    - Prioritize saving and investing over impulsive spending.
    - Create and follow a financial plan that aligns with your goals.
3. Long-Term Focus:
    - Resist the temptation of short-term gains at the expense of long-term security.
    - Regularly revisit your financial goals to ensure they remain relevant and achievable.
4. Adaptability:

- Be prepared to adjust your strategies in response to life changes or economic shifts.
- Embrace innovation and explore new tools or methods to manage your wealth.

Habits to Sustain Wealth

1. Consistent Saving and Investing:
    - Automate contributions to savings and investment accounts.
    - Reinvest earnings to benefit from compound growth.
2. Budget Management:
    - Monitor and adjust your budget to reflect changes in income or expenses.
    - Avoid lifestyle inflation by living within your means, even as wealth grows.
3. Risk Awareness:
    - Regularly assess your financial risks and take steps to mitigate them.
    - Diversify investments to protect against market volatility.
4. Debt Avoidance:
    - Minimize debt by prioritizing cash payments and avoiding high-interest loans.
    - Use credit wisely, ensuring that any borrowing aligns with your financial plan.

Cultivating a Wealth-Sustaining Mindset

A positive financial mindset is rooted in self-awareness and intentionality. Steps to cultivate this mindset include:

1. Set Clear Values:
    - Identify the values that drive your financial decisions, such as security, generosity, or freedom.
    - Ensure that your actions align with these

values.
2. Practice Gratitude:
   - Focus on the progress you've made and the resources you have.
   - Gratitude helps prevent envy or fear of loss, fostering a healthier relationship with money.
3. Seek Accountability:
   - Share your financial goals with a trusted friend, advisor, or mentor.
   - Regular check-ins encourage and keep you on track.
4. Embrace Continuous Learning:
   - Dedicate time to improving your financial knowledge through books, courses, or seminars.
   - Stay curious and open to new ideas.

Avoiding Wealth Erosion

Even substantial wealth can erode without proper management. Common causes include:
- Unnecessary Spending: Resist the urge to overspend on luxuries or nonessential items.
- Lack of Planning: Failing to plan for taxes, estate distribution, or unexpected events can lead to significant losses.
- Ignoring Inflation: Ensure that your investments outpace inflation to preserve purchasing power.
- Emotional Decision-Making: Avoid making financial choices based on fear, greed, or peer pressure.

Action Steps

1. Revisit Goals: Review your financial goals and ensure they align with your long-term vision.
2. Track Progress: Use tools or spreadsheets to monitor savings, investments, and expenses.

3. Identify Risks: Conduct a risk assessment and take steps to mitigate potential challenges.
4. Invest in Growth: Dedicate resources to learning new skills or exploring innovative opportunities.
5. Reflect Regularly: Schedule time to evaluate your financial mindset and adjust as needed.

Closing Reflection

Sustaining wealth is a lifelong endeavor that requires intentionality, discipline, and a willingness to adapt. By cultivating a mindset focused on growth and long-term success, you can protect your financial achievements and create a lasting legacy.

Take a moment to reflect: How can you strengthen your financial habits and mindset to sustain your wealth over the long term?

Inspirational Thought

"Wealth consists not in having great possessions, but in having few wants." —Epictetus

CHAPTER 15: THE POWER OF GIVING BACK

Wealth is not just about what you accumulate; it's also about how you use it to make a difference. Giving back creates a ripple effect, positively impacting your community while enriching your life with purpose and fulfillment. In this chapter, we will explore the benefits of generosity, strategies for meaningful giving, and how to align your philanthropic efforts with your values.

Why Giving Back Matters

Generosity has a profound impact on both the giver and the receiver. Benefits include:

- Strengthened Communities: Your contributions can fund programs, services, or initiatives that improve lives.
- Personal Fulfillment: Giving back fosters a sense of purpose and gratitude.
- Legacy Building: Philanthropy allows you to create a lasting impact that reflects your values.
- Networking Opportunities: Engaging in charitable work often connects you with like-minded individuals and organizations.

Forms of Giving Back

There are many ways to give back, each with its unique impact.

Consider these options:

1. Financial Contributions:
   - Donate to charities, non-profits, or community organizations that align with your values.
   - Set up recurring donations to ensure consistent support.
2. Volunteer Work:
   - Offer your time and skills to causes you care about, such as mentoring, teaching, or community service.
3. In-Kind Donations:
   - Provide goods or services to those in need, such as clothing, food, or professional expertise.
4. Establishing Foundations:
   - Create a family foundation or trust to support charitable causes on a larger scale.
5. Mentorship:
   - Please share your knowledge and experience to guide others on their journey, whether professionally or personally.

Aligning Giving with Your Values

To make your contributions meaningful, align them with your core values and passions. Steps to achieve this include:

1. Identify Causes You Care About:
   - Reflect on issues or communities that resonate with you, such as education, healthcare, or environmental conservation.
2. Research Organizations:
   - Ensure the organizations you support are reputable and aligned with your values by reviewing their mission, financial transparency, and impact reports.
3. Set Goals:
   - Define what you hope to achieve through

your giving, whether it's funding scholarships, building infrastructure, or supporting policy changes.

Strategic Philanthropy

Approach your giving with the same intention and planning as other financial decisions. Strategies include:

- Budget for Giving: Allocate a portion of your income or wealth specifically for charitable contributions.
- Tax-Efficient Giving: Consult with a financial advisor to take advantage of tax deductions for charitable donations.
- Partner with Others: Collaborate with friends, family, or organizations to amplify your impact.
- Measure Impact: Regularly evaluate the outcomes of your contributions to ensure they align with your goals.

Teaching Generosity

Instilling the value of giving back to future generations ensures that your legacy of generosity continues. Ways to teach this include:

- Involve Your Family: Include children or loved ones in charitable giving and volunteering discussions.
- Lead by Example: Demonstrate generosity through your actions.
- Create Traditions: Establish family traditions, such as annual donation drives or volunteer days.
- Encourage Creativity: Allow younger family members to choose causes or projects they are passionate about.

Action Steps

1. Reflect on Values: Identify causes or issues that align with your passions.
2. Research Opportunities: Look into organizations or

initiatives that need support.
3. Budget for Giving: Set aside a specific amount or percentage of your income for charitable contributions.
4. Volunteer Your Time: Find opportunities to share your skills or time with your community.
5. Track Impact: Evaluate the outcomes of your giving and adjust your approach as needed.

Closing Reflection

Giving back is one of the most rewarding aspects of building wealth. By aligning your contributions with your values and strategically approaching generosity, you can create a legacy that uplifts others while enriching your life.

Take a moment to reflect: How can you use your resources and skills to make a meaningful difference in your community?

Inspirational Thought

"No one has ever become poor by giving." —Anne Frank.

CHAPTER 16: EMBRACING YOUR FINANCIAL JOURNEY

Your financial journey is uniquely yours, shaped by your experiences, challenges, and goals. Embracing it fully means acknowledging your progress, learning from setbacks, and celebrating every step forward. This chapter serves as a reminder to approach your financial path with patience, determination, and gratitude, while continuously striving for growth.

Reflecting on Your Progress

Reflecting on how far you've come is essential for maintaining motivation and perspective.

Consider these steps:

1. Review Milestones:
   - Look back at your achievements, such as paying off debt, building savings, or reaching investment goals.
2. Acknowledge Growth:
   - Recognize how your financial knowledge, habits, and mindset have evolved.
3. Learn from Challenges:
   - Analyze past setbacks to identify lessons and avoid repeating mistakes.
4. Celebrate Wins:

- Reward yourself for progress, no matter how small, to reinforce positive behaviors.

The Power of Patience

Building wealth and financial stability takes time. Cultivating patience is not a sign of weakness, but a powerful tool that allows you to stay focused on long-term goals rather than becoming discouraged by short-term obstacles.

- Trust the Process: Remember that small, consistent actions compound over time.
- Focus on Progress: Shift your attention from perfection to continuous improvement.
- Stay Disciplined: Stick to your financial plan even when results materialize.

Overcoming Financial Comparison

Comparing your journey to others can lead to unnecessary stress and feelings of inadequacy. Strategies to avoid comparison include:

- Focus on Your Goals: Prioritize what matters most instead of measuring yourself against others.
- Limit Social Media Exposure: Avoid platforms that promote unrealistic financial expectations.
- Practice Gratitude: Shift your focus to what you have achieved rather than what you lack.

Staying Committed to Growth

Personal and financial growth is a lifelong process. Commit to continuous learning and adaptability by:

1. Setting New Goals: Revisit and update your financial objectives as your circumstances evolve.
2. Seeking Knowledge: Explore books, courses, and mentors to deepen your understanding of personal finance.

3. Taking Calculated Risks: Step out of your comfort zone to seize opportunities for advancement.
4. Staying Resilient: Embrace change and uncertainty as opportunities for growth rather than setbacks.

Gratitude and Giving Back

Gratitude enriches your financial journey, fostering a positive mindset and deepening your purpose. Combine gratitude with giving back to make your journey even more meaningful:

- Reflect Daily: Take a moment each day to appreciate your progress and the resources you have.
- Support Others: Share your knowledge or resources to uplift those around you.
- Create Impact: Align your financial goals with causes that resonate with your values.

Action Steps

1. Write Your Story: Create a journal entry summarizing your financial journey, highlighting milestones and lessons learned.
2. Set a Vision: Define what success looks like for you in the next five or ten years.
3. Practice Gratitude: List three things you're grateful for about your finances.
4. Identify Growth Areas: Choose one aspect of your financial habits or knowledge to improve.
5. Share Your Journey: Inspire others by sharing your experiences and strategies.

Closing Reflection

Your financial journey is not just about numbers; it's about the person you become. You can achieve economic stability and fulfillment by embracing the process, practicing patience, and maintaining a growth-oriented mindset. Remember, every step forward is a victory worth celebrating.

Take a moment to reflect: How can you embrace and celebrate your financial journey while continuing to strive for growth?

Inspirational Thought

"The journey of a thousand miles begins with a single step." —Lao Tzu.

www.ingramcontent.com/pod-product-compliance
Lightning Source LLC
Chambersburg PA
CBHW071425220526
45469CB00004B/1434